Fraser Valley Elementary School

551.57 HIR
Hirschmann, Kris, 19   It's wet out!

T 3000922

It's Wet Out!

Kris Hirschmann

ABDO
Publishing Company

visit us at
www.abdopublishing.com

Published by ABDO Publishing Company, 8000 West 78th Street, Edina, Minnesota 55439.
Copyright © 2008 by Abdo Consulting Group, Inc. International copyrights reserved in all
countries. No part of this book may be reproduced in any form without written permission from the
publisher. The Checkerboard Library™ is a trademark and logo of ABDO Publishing Company.

Printed in the United States.

Cover Photo: Getty Images
Interior Photos: AP Images pp. 15, 23, 27, 29; Getty Images pp. 1, 5; iStockphoto pp. 8, 10, 25, 29;
    Kenneth G. Libbrecht/SnowCrystals.com p. 19; National Oceanic and Atmospheric
    Administration/Department of Commerce p. 9; Peter Arnold pp. 17, 21

Series Coordinator: Megan M. Gunderson
Editors: Megan M. Gunderson, BreAnn Rumsch
Art Direction & Cover Design: Neil Klinepier

Library of Congress Cataloging-in-Publication Data

Hirschmann, Kris, 1967-
  It's wet out! / Kris Hirschmann.
     p. cm. -- (What's it like out?)
  Includes bibliographical references and index.
  ISBN 978-1-59928-944-1
  1. Precipitation (Meteorology)--Juvenile literature. 2. Rain and rainfall--Juvenile literature. 3.
Hydrologic cycle--Juvenile literature. I. Title.

  QC920.H57 2008
  551.57'7--dc22

                                     2007029155

Contents

It's Wet Out!

Imagine you are playing outdoors. When you went outside, the sun was shining brightly. But now, gray clouds are rolling in. "I wonder if I should go inside?" you think as the sun disappears.

Just then, a raindrop hits your cheek. The first drop is followed by another, and then another. You bolt for your house just in time! As you reach your front porch, the skies open up. Water streams down in sheets, drenching everything it touches. There's no doubt about it, it's wet out!

Most people have seen this kind of **cloudburst**. But gray skies do not always bring downpours. They may produce light drizzle, steady rain, hail, sleet, freezing rain, or snow. All of these things are called precipitation. They look different from each other, but they have something in common. They are all forms of moisture that fall from the sky.

Will rain delay your game today?

Or, will you go out in the rain to play?

Into the Sky

Before moisture can fall from the sky, it has to get into the sky. The first step in this process is called **evaporation**. Evaporation occurs when the sun heats the earth's oceans, lakes, streams, and other bodies of water.

As water heats up, its molecules start to zip around more quickly. Some molecules at the water's surface break away from the others and fly into the air. They turn into an invisible gas called water vapor.

Evaporation from bodies of water provides about 90 percent of the moisture in Earth's atmosphere. Ten percent comes from transpiration. This is what happens when water evaporates from plants.

Water vapor enters the air near ground level. But sometimes, it gets carried upward with warm air. This happens through convection, when warm air rises from the ground like an invisible hot-air balloon. It also happens when warm air flows up over mountains or ridges through orographic (awr-uh-GRA-fihk) lifting.

Warm air may also rise through frontal lifting when **air masses** meet. Or, air may be forced upward when it converges on the same area. Rising air can travel high into the sky, taking a load of water vapor with it.

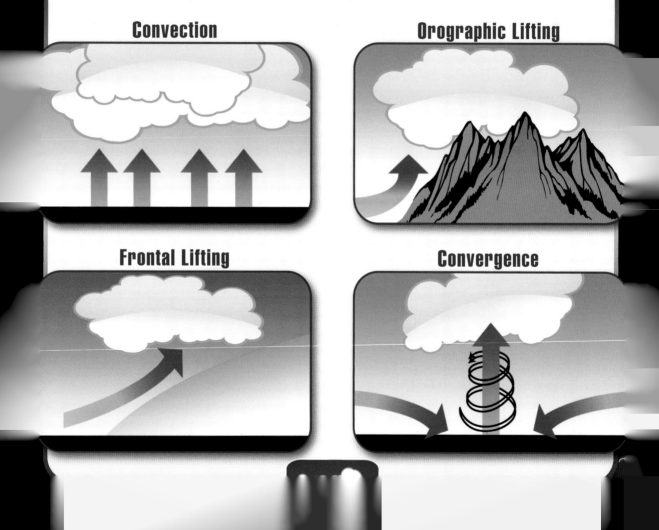

Convection

Orographic Lifting

Frontal Lifting

Convergence

Condensation

Rising air doesn't just carry water vapor. It also carries tiny pieces of dust, salt, and other matter. These particles are too small to see with the naked eye. Yet they are there, and there are lots of them! In fact, you may suck in several hundred thousand particles each time you take a breath.

As warm, moist air rises, it expands and cools. As the temperature drops below the **dew point**, the air becomes supersaturated. At this point, the air is holding more than its **capacity** of water vapor. So, water vapor starts **condensing** onto those solid particles in the air. The particles are called cloud condensation nuclei. Clouds would not form without them!

A cold drink causes water vapor in the air near the glass to cool below the dew point. This causes condensation you can see at ground level!

How the water vapor behaves at this stage depends on the air temperature. Above 32 degrees Fahrenheit (0°C), water vapor **condenses** back into liquid water droplets. Below this temperature, water vapor can experience **sublimation** instead. It hardens directly into ice crystals. Either way, the water vapor turns into visible particles. These particles float together in a white clump called a cloud.

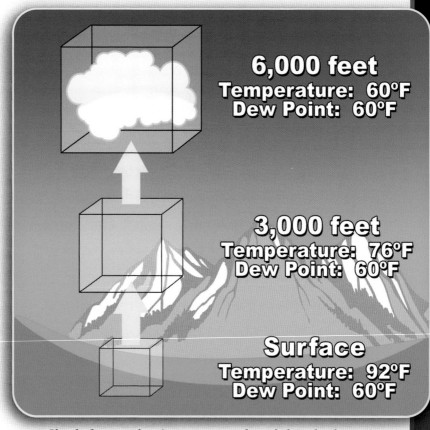

6,000 feet
Temperature: 60°F
Dew Point: 60°F

3,000 feet
Temperature: 76°F
Dew Point: 60°F

Surface
Temperature: 92°F
Dew Point: 60°F

Clouds form as the air temperature drops below the dew point.

Making Raindrops

Newly formed cloud droplets are very tiny. They measure just 0.0004 inches (0.01 mm) across. They are much too light to fall to the ground. So, they drift gently within the cloud and float wherever breezes push them.

Over time, the cloud droplets grow and grow. More water vapor **condenses** onto the droplets. Then, the droplets may bump into each other and stick together. If they become heavy enough, they will start falling toward the ground. This is the beginning of a rain shower.

In clouds, both water droplets and ice crystals create rain. Water droplets may coalesce (koh-uh-LEHS), or combine, to form raindrops. Eventually, they become too heavy for the air to hold them up. Then, the rain begins falling.

Will you be prepared when the rain starts falling?

RAINDROP FORMATION

Ice Crystals to Rain

ICE CRYSTAL COLLECTS WATER VAPOR

CRYSTALS COLLIDE AND FORM SNOWFLAKE

SNOWFLAKE MELTS IN WARMER TEMPERATURES

RAINDROP FALLS

Droplets to Rain

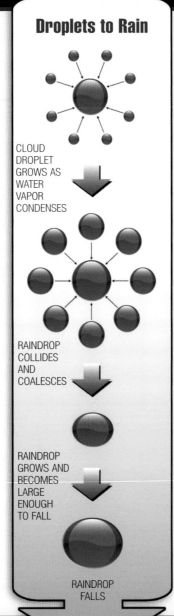

CLOUD DROPLET GROWS AS WATER VAPOR CONDENSES

RAINDROP COLLIDES AND COALESCES

RAINDROP GROWS AND BECOMES LARGE ENOUGH TO FALL

RAINDROP FALLS

If a cloud has ice crystals, water vapor may collect on the ice crystals to make them grow. These ice crystals may also **merge** to form snowflakes. The crystals or snowflakes melt when they fall into air that is above 32 degrees Fahrenheit (0°C). So by the time they reach the ground, they have turned into liquid raindrops.

About 1 million cloud droplets form one small raindrop!

Looking at Raindrops

Precipitation comes in many sizes. The smallest forms are about 0.01 to 0.02 inches (0.2 to 0.5 mm) across. Liquid precipitation of this size is called drizzle. It travels at about 30 to 80 inches per second (700 to 2,000 mm/s). And, the droplets stay round as they fall.

Raindrops are larger than drizzle. If they are about .04 inches (1 mm) in size, they also stay round. An average raindrop is about .08 inches (2 mm) across. Drops of this size and larger fall faster. They also lose their shape as they fall. Air flowing past the drops forces them to flatten until they look like the top halves of hamburger buns.

The largest raindrops are about .25 inches (6 mm) across. Big raindrops can travel at speeds of more than 20 miles per hour (32 km/h)! They bend upward in the middle, forming tiny parachutes as they fall. As they plummet toward the ground, these larger raindrops may break apart into smaller drops.

Raindrop size depends on the conditions inside a cloud. Sometimes, a cloud develops strong updrafts. These upward-flowing air currents keep raindrops **circulating** in the cloud. The stronger the updraft, the larger a raindrop must grow before becoming heavy enough to fall.

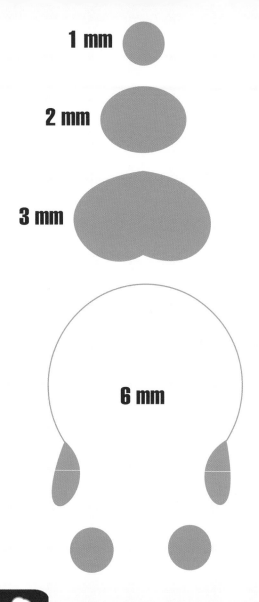

1 mm

2 mm

3 mm

6 mm

The bigger the raindrop, the more it is affected by the air it falls through. Tiny drops stay round. When raindrops get too large, the parachute shape breaks apart to form smaller drops.

Hail

In some storm clouds, updrafts become very strong. They blast frozen raindrops called hail **embryos** high into cold areas of the cloud. Along the way, **supercooled** water droplets strike the surface of the embryos. This makes the embryos grow in size and become hailstones.

Eventually, the hailstones become too heavy for the updrafts to keep them aloft. At this point, they fall out of the cloud and plunge to the ground.

Most hailstones are less than one inch (2.5 cm) across. But some hailstones become much larger. Very strong updrafts allow big hailstones to form. Under these conditions, hailstones can stay in a cloud for a long time without falling. Over and over, they **circulate** up and down in the cloud.

With each trip, a hailstone develops a new ice layer. Hailstones freeze at different rates depending on where they are in the cloud. This is because of temperature differences within a cloud. The process gives the ice alternating clear and white layers. By the time a hailstone finally leaves the cloud, it may be as big as a softball!

In the United States and Canada, most hailstorms occur in spring and summer. A large hailstorm can cover an area with icy drifts. These drifts may change a green summer landscape into a winter wonderland!

The largest U.S. hailstone on record fell in Coffeyville, Kansas, in 1970. It weighed 1.67 pounds (.76 kg) and measured 5.7 inches (14.5 cm) across. However, a hailstone of unknown weight measuring 7 inches (18 cm) across fell in Aurora, Nebraska, in 2003.

Meteorologists often refer to the size of hailstones by comparing them to common objects.

NAME - SIZE IN INCHES
Pea — .25
Marble or Mothball — .50
Penny or Dime — .75
Nickel — .88
Quarter — 1.00
Half-Dollar — 1.25
Walnut or Ping-Pong Ball — 1.50
Golf Ball — 1.75
Hen's Egg — 2.00
Tennis Ball — 2.50
Baseball — 2.75
Teacup — 3.00
Grapefruit — 4.00
Softball — 4.50

Sleet and Freezing Rain

Hailstones are not the only form of ice that falls from the sky. During the winter, icy pellets called sleet may also strike the earth. Sleet begins when a cloud floats on a shallow layer of warm air. When snow leaves the cloud, it partly melts in that warmer layer.

Next, the partially melted drops fall through a deeper cold air layer below. This freezes the precipitation solid again. Then, the frozen drops reach the ground as sleet.

Sometimes, the warm air layer is deeper and the cold air layer is shallower. In these cases, freezing rain may form instead of sleet. Falling snowflakes melt in the deeper warm layer of air. But the chilly layer is smaller. So, the melted snowflakes make it all the way to the ground without turning back into ice.

Long episodes of accumulating freezing rain are called ice storms. They can leave behind a beautiful, sparkly landscape. But, large amounts of ice can create dangerous conditions.

But, these drops are still **supercooled** when they reach ground level. There, objects may be below freezing. In this case, the raindrops spread out and refreeze the instant they land.

Freezing rain can be very dangerous. It topples trees, snaps telephone and power lines, and blankets streets and sidewalks with ice. Until the ice melts, people may have a hard time getting around.

Snow

Snow is another type of falling ice. But unlike hail, sleet, and freezing rain, snow is usually soft and gentle. Many people look forward to winter's first snowfall.

Snow develops similarly to rain. Between -40 degrees Fahrenheit (-40°C) and 32 degrees Fahrenheit (0°C), **supercooled** water may freeze into ice crystals. This happens if it comes into contact with freezing, or ice, nuclei. These are similar to **condensation** nuclei. Below -40 degrees Fahrenheit, water vapor may form directly into ice crystals.

Like raindrops, snowflakes come in many sizes. When conditions are very cold, there is not much extra moisture in the air. So, snowflakes tend to be tiny. But at warmer temperatures, more water vapor joins the ice crystals. They may also collide with other crystals to form larger snowflakes. This process is called aggregation.

When the crystals get heavy enough, they drift downward out of the cloud. If the crystals reach warm air below the cloud, they melt into raindrops. But if temperatures are below the freezing point, the crystals stay solid. Eventually, snowflakes reach the ground.

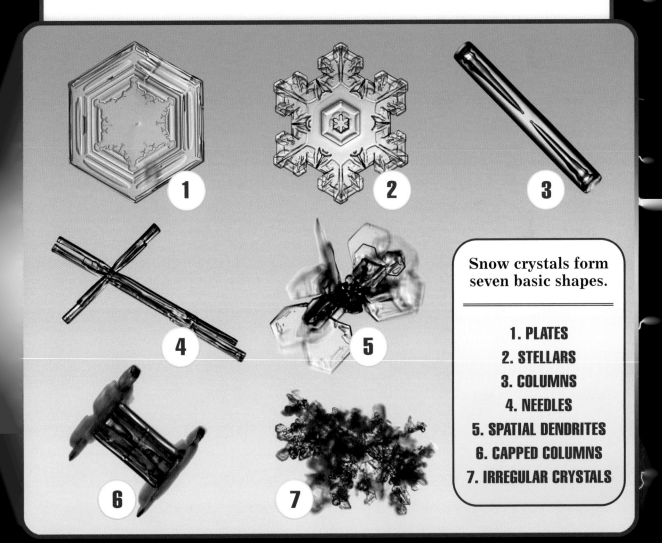

Snow crystals form seven basic shapes.

1. PLATES
2. STELLARS
3. COLUMNS
4. NEEDLES
5. SPATIAL DENDRITES
6. CAPPED COLUMNS
7. IRREGULAR CRYSTALS

How Much Precipitation?

Snow, rain, and other types of precipitation do not just come in different sizes. They also come in different quantities. Large clouds formed in unstable conditions can dump huge amounts of precipitation.

How much precipitation do clouds produce? To measure rain, scientists collect it in tube-shaped **gauges** with funnels at the top. Then, they look at the inch or millimeter markings on the rain gauge. This reveals how much rain fell during a certain time period.

For snow, a simple ruler shows you how much has fallen. To find an area's average snow depth, spread out many rulers and take several measurements. This is called a snow course.

Rainfall and snowfall are described as light, moderate, or heavy. For rain, the amount that falls in a certain period of time determines the category. Up to .10 inches (.25 cm) in an hour qualifies as light rain. More than .30 inches (.76 cm) in an hour is heavy rainfall. This rain may fall so heavily you won't even be able to identify individual drops!

For snow, visibility determines the category. In light snowfall, you can see farther than one-half mile (.8 km) in front of you. In heavy snowfall, you can't see farther than one-quarter mile (.4 km).

To obtain precise readings, rain gauges should be placed away from wind and objects such as trees.

Extreme Precipitation

Many storms are moderate, but some are much worse. Blizzards and severe thunderstorms can be especially dangerous. They can bring massive amounts of rain and snow.

In the United States, thunderstorms usually occur during spring and summer. They form when warm air carries a lot of water vapor into the sky. When conditions in the atmosphere are unstable, **condensing** water vapor grows into huge clouds called thunderheads.

Thunderheads produce wind, lightning, thunder, hail, and buckets of rain. A severe thunderstorm can drop 4.7 inches (12 cm) of rain in just 20 minutes!

Blizzards take place during winter. These storms feature low temperatures, whipping winds, and heavy, blowing snow. They can harm people, plants, and animals. Blizzards can

Officially, a blizzard has 35 mile-per-hour (56 km/h) winds. Visibility may be less than .25 miles (.4 km). These conditions may call for a blizzard warning to be issued. A ground blizzard warning is issued when blowing, drifting, fallen snow causes blizzardlike conditions.

also damage property and bring business to a halt. For this reason, blizzards are costly. For example, a blizzard that struck the U.S. East Coast in 1993 caused about $3 billion in damage.

On the Ground

Whether they are light or heavy, all storms have an important job. They remove water from the air and return it to Earth's surface as part of the hydrologic cycle. This is the process of how water moves across Earth from oceans to clouds to land and back again.

Nearly 80 percent of all precipitation falls into Earth's oceans. The rest falls onto land. When it does, it often soaks right into the ground. This process is called infiltration. After infiltration, water may stay in the soil as ground moisture. Or, it may drip farther underground.

Sometimes precipitation cannot sink into soil. This can happen when the soil is already full of moisture. Other times, water falls faster than the ground can absorb it. Under these conditions, **runoff** flows across Earth's surface. It trickles downhill until it reaches streams, rivers, or lakes. From there, it may travel all the way to the ocean to begin the process again.

The Hydrologic Cycle

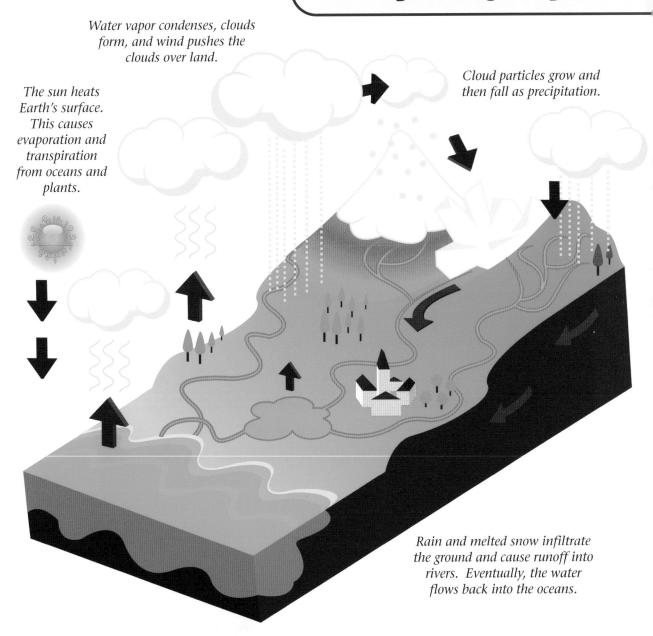

Water vapor condenses, clouds form, and wind pushes the clouds over land.

Cloud particles grow and then fall as precipitation.

The sun heats Earth's surface. This causes evaporation and transpiration from oceans and plants.

Rain and melted snow infiltrate the ground and cause runoff into rivers. Eventually, the water flows back into the oceans.

Floods

Runoff can get very heavy if a great deal of precipitation falls. Waterlogged soil and large quantities of melting snow can also increase runoff. The runoff can swell rivers and streams. It can even force them to overflow their banks. This situation is called a flood.

Some floods form during long periods of rain or snow. During these periods, water levels rise throughout several days. This often gives people plenty of warning that a flood is on its way. They may not be able to stop the water from coming. But, they often have time to move to safety.

A slow-moving flood can last for weeks. The water can creep into homes, soak farmland, wash away streets, and shut down businesses. It can cause billions of dollars in damage.

Not all floods form slowly. Some form very quickly and are incredibly dangerous. The fastest-rising flood of all is

A flood watch means flooding is possible in a certain area. A flood warning means flooding is or will soon be occurring. Know your area's flood risk so you can evacuate safely, if necessary.

called a flash flood. It occurs when **runoff** from a slow-moving storm flows into a narrow area. The runoff gets squeezed into a rushing wall of water. It can sweep away people, animals, cars, and anything else in its path.

Droughts

The opposite of floods are dry periods called droughts (DROWTS). Droughts develop when rainfall and snowfall are lighter than usual over a long period of time. During a drought, water **evaporates** from the ground without being replaced by precipitation. Lakes, rivers, and streams begin to dry up. The ground may even harden and crack.

Severe droughts can cause crop failure over large areas. When this happens, agriculture is devastated. Farmers lose their businesses, and people can't get enough food. In some nations, millions of people have starved to death during droughts.

Droughts remind us that rain, snow, and other types of precipitation are very important. They are a vital part of nature's balance. So don't feel gloomy when the skies turn gray. Just smile as you say, "It's wet out!"

Above-average temperatures are common during a drought. They can contribute to crop damage. And, forest and grass fires occur more often and spread more quickly during drought conditions.

Glossary

air mass - a large body of air containing nearly uniform temperature and humidity.

capacity - the maximum amount of something that can be held or contained.

circulate - to move in a circle, especially to follow a repeating course.

cloudburst - a sudden, heavy rainfall.

condense - to change from a gas or a vapor into a liquid or a solid, usually caused by a decrease in temperature.

dew point - the temperature at which water vapor begins condensing.

embryo - something in the early stages of development.

evaporate - to change from a liquid or a solid into a vapor.

gauge - a measuring device.

merge - to combine or blend.

runoff - water, such as rain, that runs or flows off land into streams or other bodies of water.

sublimate - to change from a solid to a vapor without going through a liquid phase. Also, to condense directly back into a solid from a vapor.

supercooled - relating to when a liquid, such as water, remains liquid below its freezing point.

Web Sites

To learn more about weather, visit ABDO Publishing Company on the World Wide Web at **www.abdopublishing.com**. Web sites about weather are featured on our Book Links page. These links are routinely monitored and updated to provide the most current information available.

Index